My Desk Is Driving Me Crazy

"Wow, do I wish I would have had this book in my twenties! *My Desk Is Driving Me Crazy* is filled with wisdom that is both practical and transformational, just like its author, Sue Rasmussen. I've turned to her so many times for direction and she's always been able to focus, simply and immediately, on the core issue. Her seven radical principles of ease and clarity will help you do the same thing for yourself. This is an enjoyable and accessible guide to clearing the inner and outer clutter that gets in the way of the life for which you're longing."

—**Kimberly Schneider**, M.Ed., JD, LPC, author of
Everything You Need Is Right Here:
Five Steps to Manifesting Magic and Miracles

"I love this book. Sue has taken a struggle so common it is widely accepted as *the* normal state of being and flipped it. What if the norm is actively preventing us from achieving our hearts desire? What if doing less really does accomplish more? Why is 'free time' considered a luxury or a sign of weakness vs. an essential step in the creative process? We advise people to 'sleep on it' when faced with a difficult problem. What if the same methodology was approached while we are awake? This book is for everyone who has felt the pinch of never-ending emails, projects, and to-do lists and who strives for that sense of inner balance. It offers a way to reconnect to the person who had a passion that ignited a career path. Learn how to let go. Read this book...and give yourself the break you deserve."

—**Tracy McCrory**, Project Manager

"WOW! I just finished *My Desk Is Driving Me Crazy* (first, I had to quiet my inner monkey mind telling me that I didn't have time to read this book and that I had way too much to get done on my long to-do list first). I love this book! So many good ideas, and they go against a lot of what we've been taught in today's business. Sue Rasmussen's unexpected approach – work less to get more accomplished – who knew? Even though it is written for women, I'm going to share it with the men in my life, too. A must read for anyone who has too much to do in an ever-increasing and fast-paced world!"

—**Jenny Karos**, Promotions Supervisor

"I read *My Desk Is Driving Me Crazy* in one sitting! I couldn't put it down. This easy-to-read, practical book not only simplified how to manage my desk, but how to bring order and sanity into my life! It's a must read for any entrepreneur who struggles with managing time or deals with overwhelm and stress. Sue Rasmussen's book will revolutionize your thinking about career and life!"

—**Cherry Norris**, actor, director of *Duty Dating*

"In *My Desk Is Driving Me Crazy*, Sue Rasmussen leads us smoothly through the thorny thickets of 'to dos' and 'must dos.' The other side is amazing as life opens up to the creative joys of time and energy, owned, used and guided by ME and my own sense of what's best for me. This is how I always knew life should be but could never find my way there. Sue has given me a great gift by showing me the way."

—**Susan Stevens**, LCSW

"Although written with the small business owner in mind, this book really speaks to anyone seeking success in business, or even their personal life! If you've ever struggled with putting yourself first, prioritizing what you want most, or checking everything off your to-do list, *My Desk Is Driving Me Crazy* is a helpful form of both advice and counseling. Written in a friendly, approachable manner, you'll likely find yourself saying 'Yes, that's me!' repeatedly. This could almost be a companion piece to the popular *StrengthsFinder* business series. Sue Rasmussen asks us to consider whether we should be working harder to keep earning ourselves 'gold stars,' or working smarter to achieve better results and happier selves. Seems like a more than valid question, and I can't wait to implement the strategies in my work and see what unfolds. If you need a little Zen in your type-A life, this might be just the ticket!"

—**Amy Hodge Schulz**, Marketing Strategist

"We're so used to everything being 'right now' because of how social media and technology has changed us. We even check work email while we're on vacation, just to make sure everything is okay. I laughed out loud reading this book; it nails the different ways we rush through the day, constantly rehashing our list of things to get done. Sue Rasmussen's book gives us permission to unplug, quiet the Monkey Mind, and start listening to our inner wisdom instead. Yes, even at work."

—**Colleen Lennartson,**
Senior Operations Accountant

"I highly recommend *My Desk is Driving Me Crazy* to an expanded audience; any life stage, male or female, home, corporate, small business or entrepreneur. The vision is timeless and the writing is clear, unambiguous, actionable and practical. Sue Rasmussen takes ageless and proven monastic principles and applies them to productivity and clarity for the entrepreneur. It seems counter intuitive for those of us driven to "do" to stop, open our hearts and souls to listen. Living this new lifestyle will blossom to a less cluttered and overwhelmed life by focusing on the truly important."

—**Margit Tritt**, Product Manager and Consultant

"Once again, Sue Rasmussen offers her laser clarity and practical suggestions for easing up on overwhelm... all in an easy-to-read, very user-friendly, and inspirational manner. Thank you, Sue!"

—**Sara E.**, artist

"*My Desk Is Driving Me Crazy* offers a refreshing take on the things we *think* make us unproductive in our work and personal lives. Sue Rasmussen explains why the daily physical and mental clutter holds us back and how to remove those problems from your life forever. After reading just a few pages I felt myself relax and knew I could start making the changes to improve my life immediately. Make time to read this book and you'll get it back tenfold."

—**Gina Catalano**, Business Coach
and author of *Tandem Leadership*

"Busyness becomes an illness when it is not aligned with your true values and your soul. I believe our culture is experiencing this in epidemic proportions. Sue Rasmussen's *My Desk Is Driving Me Crazy* is the remedy if you are looking for more ease, more wholeness and more truth in your life. There is no other book like this and no better woman to teach this. I have had the privilege of knowing Sue's work for nearly a decade and know first-hand that she walks this path of wisdom herself. I highly recommend taking yourself from crazy to uncluttered ASAP."

—**Heather Gray**, Life Coach at **soulfilledlife.com** and award-winning co-author of *Real Girl Real World: A Guide to Finding Your True Self*

My **Desk**
Is Driving Me
Crazy

END OVERWHELM, DO LESS,
AND ACCOMPLISH MORE

SUE RASMUSSEN

NEW YORK

NASHVILLE • MELBOURNE • VANCOUVER

My Desk Is Driving Me Crazy
END OVERWHELM, DO LESS, AND ACCOMPLISH MORE

© 2017 **SUE RASMUSSEN**

Published in New York, New York, by Morgan James Publishing in partnership with Difference Press. Morgan James is a trademark of Morgan James, LLC. www.MorganJamesPublishing.com

The Morgan James Speakers Group can bring authors to your live event. For more information or to book an event visit The Morgan James Speakers Group at www.TheMorganJamesSpeakersGroup.com.

ISBN 978-1-68350-203-6 paperback
ISBN 978-1-68350-204-3 eBook
ISBN 978-1-68350-205-0 hardcover
Library of Congress Control Number:
2016914145

Cover Design by:
Megan James

Interior Design by:
Bonnie Bushman
The Whole Caboodle Graphic Design

Editing: Grace Kerina

Author's photo courtesy of Bill Raab,
Exposed to Light Photography

In an effort to support local communities, raise awareness and funds, Morgan James Publishing donates a percentage of all book sales for the life of each book to Habitat for Humanity Peninsula and Greater Williamsburg.

Get involved today! Visit
www.MorganJamesBuilds.com

Dedication

For authors who had the courage to share their stories,
messages, and paths of transformation.
Thank you. You have changed my life
in more ways than you will ever know.

Table of Contents

Introduction	**Busy, Stressed, and Overwhelmed**	**xvii**
	What It's Costing Your Business	xx
	A Vision of Ease and Clarity	xxiii
	Why Should You Believe Me?	xxiv
	The Unexpected Solution	xxviii
	The Seven Principles	xxix
Chapter 1	**Principle #1: Reconsider Being in the Know**	**1**
	FoMO: Fear of Missing Out	1
	The High Cost of Staying in the Loop	3
	Just-in-Time Learning	4
	The 30-Day Information Vacation	6
Chapter 2	**Principle #2: Get Comfortable with Time on Your Hands**	**9**
	The Seduction of Drama	10
	The "Use Time Wisely" Fallacy	11
	Brilliance Needs Breathing Room	12
	You've Got Plenty of Time	13

	Parkinson's Law	14
Chapter 3	**Principle #3: Do Less to Accomplish More**	**16**
	The "Work Harder" Fallacy	16
	The Illusion of Being Able to Do It All	18
	The 80/20 Rule	18
	The Fastest Way to Cut Through Overwhelm	20
	The Shortest To-Do List on the Planet	21
Chapter 4	**Principle #4: Make Decisions That Are Right for You**	**25**
	Your One-Two Power Pack	25
	How Your Body Talks	26
	Your Quiet Inner Voice	29
	Monkey Mind vs. Your Quiet Inner Voice	30
	Make Only the Decisions Needed Now	31
	Make Courageous Decisions	33
Chapter 5	**Principle #5: Let Go of Good to Make Room for Great**	**35**
	Holding on Means Holding Back	35
	The Sunk Cost Dilemma	38
	The Butterfly Effect of Letting Go	39
	How to Tell When It's Time to Let Go	41
	Move Some Pebbles to Move a Mountain	43

Chapter 6   **Principle #6: Blaze Your Own Trail**   **45**

Someone Else's Way May Not Be
Your Way

Impress Yourself Instead   47

The Unwanted Effects of the   49
Unspoken No

Your Vacation Self, Every Day   52

Chapter 7   **Principle #7: Lean in to Find the**   **54**
Buried Treasure

Your Next Breakthrough   54

When You Feel Confused, Go Within   55

Follow the Inklings, Even When   57
They're Scary

Your Very Own Archeological Dig   59

Dare to Be Average   61

Chapter 8   **What Could Go Wrong?**   **65**

The Rider, the Elephant, and the   65
Path Run the Show

Things Feel Worse Before They   68
Get Better

The Flood Keeps Coming   69

You Feel Guilty, Anxious, and Bored   70

Our Culture Worships Busy   71

You Are Surrounded by People With
Opinions   72

Clutter Tries to Trick You   73

	You Experience Pressure to Fit In	74
	Endless Distractions Tempt You	75
Chapter 9	**Everyday Ease, Confidence, and Clarity**	77
	Getting Started	78
	How Do *You* Approach Change?	79
	Acknowledgments	*81*
	About the Author	*83*
	Thank You	*85*

Introduction

"For so many of us – myself included – it's radical to consider that major behavioral change or significant achievements could happen not because of one's fierce will, struggle, and hard work but because we support ourselves so wisely and fully that change happens with ease."

—**Tara Mohr**, *Playing Big*

Busy, Stressed, and Overwhelmed

Does your day feel like a never-ending to-do list? Are you drowning in email? How about your desk that's piled with papers? Then there are webinars, podcasts, newsletters, social media – and the pace keeps picking up.

Maybe you don't think you'll ever get on top of things and feel in control, because life today has gotten pretty complicated.

Meet Anne. She's a coach, author, and motivational speaker. She's smart, confident, good at what she does, and helps her clients get amazing results.

But here's the thing: being busy, stressed, and overwhelmed is holding her back from the success she wants and the difference she really wants to make. And she knows it.

When she gets up in the morning, she already feels pulled in a thousand directions, looking ahead at what she knows she needs to get done that day, plus all the other things on her to-do list that she really *should* do but probably won't get done. Some days she gets so overwhelmed by where to start that she ends up doing things that don't really matter just to feel like she's getting *something* done, but she knows that's not helping her business either.

Her email inbox is full of messages that she needs to answer, and she feels drained just looking at them. So she lets them sit in her inbox, waiting for the time when, hopefully, she'll be inspired to deal with them. But, in the meantime, the number of messages keeps growing and she's starting to miss important ones because she can't keep them all straight.

Her desk is driving her crazy, too. She'd love to feel creative and inspired in her office, but most of the time she feels distracted and scattered. She's embarrassed that she's a motivational speaker who inspires others to greatness, but she's on her knees digging through a pile of papers on the floor of her office trying to find the notes for her next keynote speech.

She's also spent a lot of time and money on programs and trainings and classes and books on how to be successful in her business, and she hasn't implemented even a fraction of what she's learned. In her words: "I have shiny object syndrome. I keep signing up for teleclasses and webinars and free downloads. They make me feel busy and productive even though, when I'm done, I just add more things to my to-do list that I know I will probably never do. I feel more and more behind."

When she wakes up in the middle of the night, she lies there worrying and thinking about the things that she doesn't take time to think about during the day while she's busy. There's so much to do. She doesn't know if she'll reach her next big business goals, even though she's been working hard. Even if she *does* reach her next breakthrough, she worries it will send her over the edge from the overwhelm of the resulting expanded to-do list.

Anne knows what she wants: to be calm, confident, and on top of things; to have time in her day to be creative

xx | My Desk Is Driving Me Crazy

and innovative; and to be able to work with her clients in a state of flow, which is where she does her best work. She wants to feel focused and easily achieve results.

Does Anne's story sound familiar?

If so, take heart. I have good news for you. Work doesn't have to feel overwhelming. "Crazy busy" doesn't have to be your norm.

Even better, shifting to ease and clarity is going to be much easier than you think.

What It's Costing Your Business

When you're too busy, overwhelmed, or scattered, your business takes a huge hit. The symptoms are like a cascading waterfall, one symptom contributing to the next.

When you're overwhelmed, you don't enjoy your work as much. You started your business so that you could do more of what you loved, right? When a good part of your business life feels like you're a hamster on a wheel, flooded with information and emails and never-ending tasks and decisions that don't seem to have easy answers, the joy gets sucked out of what you're doing. You start to procrastinate. You avoid making the decisions that seem hard. You feel paralyzed, not even sure what the most important things to do are. You feel stressed and overwhelmed. You don't enjoy your clients as much.

Of course you want to reach your highest potential (and help your clients reach their full potential as well) and accomplish what you want to achieve, and yet you find yourself getting sidetracked by little things that constantly whittle away your time and energy. You wonder if you might be using your overwhelm as a way to avoid something, maybe even something you really want to accomplish.

When you're going after what is nearest and dearest to your heart, or are considering making a big change, it can feel pretty scary. Creating chaos and busyness is a culturally approved way of distracting yourself from the fear of the unknown. You may say, "I'm just too busy to work on my book right now", when, in your heart, you suspect you're just stalling.

You probably also invest regularly in your business skills, and you might find it challenging to implement much of what you learn. If you work for yourself, you have likely invested thousands of dollars in training, mentoring, coaching, and certifications. However, when you feel overwhelmed or scattered, it can be really hard to focus on the most important actions to take, so you often end up much less productive, effective, or powerful than you would like to, and that feels like throwing money right down the drain.

Even if they can't quite put their finger on what's causing it, your clients can tell that something is off, too. They can feel your overwhelm. The energy you experience around your business is the energy that goes out to your clients and your potential clients. In a very real way, a major part of what they are buying when they work with you is *you*. You model for them what's possible. If your underlying energy is overwhelm or a feeling of indecision or uncertainty, your clients are deeply affected. As a result, they may be indecisive. They may have trouble saying yes to working with you. They may quibble about your pricing. They may question what you recommend. Clients who are caught in this negative energy orbit are not likely to get the kind of results or experience the success that you know they should be getting. Even worse, they're not likely to refer you to other potential clients, either.

Last but not least, when you are overwhelmed or overly busy, your profitability is dramatically impacted. You miss opportunities – guaranteed. You may be so distracted that you don't even know when a great opportunity shows up, or you may not have the bandwidth to say yes to ideas or opportunities when they do fall in your lap.

The bottom line is that when you work for yourself, you simply can't afford to be overwhelmed, stressed, or scattered.

A Vision of Ease and Clarity

So what's possible instead?

What about waking up calm, confident, and on top of things, with plenty of time in your day for creativity, flow, and ease? What about knowing that you are focused on the few, most important things that will make a major difference for your business? What if, every morning, you clearly decide on the most important thing you want to accomplish that day, and you tackle that before you do anything else?

How about putting in fewer hours? How about using the hours you do work to do only things that you not only love, but that bring you great results as well? How about trusting that you have plenty of time to relax, knowing that relaxing is as critical to your business as your "working" time.

You have a peaceful relationship with your email inbox. Your desk makes you happy. You've become "anti-busy." You are happily ruthless about letting go of things that drain your energy, steal your time, and suck you dry.

You enjoy yourself much more. You love working with your clients, and you've become used to how easy it feels. You make decisions that are authentic to your core, and you base your choices on what brings you joy and increases your energy. You easily choose the opportunities and clients and projects that are right for you, and let go of all the rest. You do things your way. Your clients sense your authenticity and ease and are drawn to you.

Best of all, you accomplish far more than you ever imagined. You no longer focus on crossing tasks off your to-do list – in fact, you rarely even have a to-do list anymore – but you get better results, period, with a lot less effort.

Does that sound good? You can create that life of ease and clarity. I'll show you how.

Why Should You Believe Me?

It's taken me years to figure out everything I'll be sharing with you here. I come from a solid, hardworking Midwestern background, and I've had to revisit almost everything I thought I knew about how to operate.

I'd always prided myself on "working hard to do things right." First in school, then at different jobs over the years, I did my best to follow the rules, do what was expected, and get the job done.

Straight As on my report cards? Check.
Manage my time well? Check.
Be hyper-organized? Check.
Get things done? Check.
Get promoted? Check.

Following those rules worked well, right up until I decided to start my own business as a coach... and then working for myself knocked me on my ass. There were no rules anymore. No teacher. No boss. Nobody to tell me what success looked like or how to make sure I did what was expected. I didn't know how to structure my own day. I worried that I wouldn't know how to work with my clients. I felt like a fraud.

There was so much to learn and to do, and I was determined to succeed. I signed up for every business success and coaching newsletter I could find. I signed up for every class and training I could squeeze in. I hired my first coach.

But I was completely overwhelmed. Every day, I felt more and more behind. Every time I received a newsletter filled with amazing tips, I added more items to my to-do list – the one that was already five pages long. Some days I'd sit at my computer and feel absolutely frozen, paralyzed with indecision. My desk was piled with papers. My filing cabinet bulged and my bookcases were filled with enormous ring binders of notes from classes and conferences. There was so much to do. I had no idea where to even start.

On one of my calls with my coach, I mentioned that I was feeling overwhelmed. She asked me to walk her through everything I was in the process of doing, everything I was reading, the classes I was taking, and what was on my to-do list. I ran through my enormous list with her, proud of myself for how dedicated I was. I was sure she was going to compliment me or tell me how great I was doing. I wanted an "A" for my massive effort. I was excited, too, because I thought she would help me create a strategic time-management plan for how I'd get it all done. I was ready, pen in hand.

Imagine my shock when, instead, she asked me to remove myself from every email list and to not take any other trainings (other than my coaching training courses) for the next *year*. All I could think was, "*What*?! But I *need* all of that information to be successful! Is she crazy?!? I'm all *about* hard work... and that's what it takes, isn't it?"

But she insisted. She told me I wasn't going to succeed going about it the way I had been.

Even though her suggestions didn't make sense to me, I remembered that I was *paying* her to coach me. I decided I had to be willing to step outside – way outside – of my comfort zone and listen to what she said.

I took her advice, and I have been eternally grateful ever since.

It wasn't easy, especially at first. I really struggled with the idea of doing less to accomplish more, and her advice shook me to the core, even though I *wanted* to believe her.

I took myself off all the mailing lists. I cut way back on what I was trying to do each day, and instead focused on the next actions that actually made sense for me. I started to cull and prioritize the notes and trainings and tips I had filed away.

My email inbox became easily manageable. I could see the surface of my desk again.

I started to get very selective about the actions I took, the people I regularly hung around with, and the information I gathered and implemented.

I learned to ignore the noise of everything that was clamoring for my attention.

I started to breathe again. I regained clarity about what I wanted to accomplish. I reconnected with the joy of working for myself. I got the right things done, and I got them done easily.

As my coaching business grew, I noticed, over and over, that my clients were struggling with the same things I had struggled with. Those business owners – smart, motivated, creative women who cared deeply about their businesses, their messages, and their clients – weren't making the kind of progress they thought they should be making, because they were often overwhelmed, way too busy, and stressed out. They often felt bad about the progress they wanted to make but weren't making. Even with all the pressure they put on themselves, they still weren't moving forward the way they wanted to. Their overwhelm was blocking their ability to create the results they wanted.

That sounded all too familiar.

As my clients and I worked together to shift them from overwhelm to ease, they started achieving their business goals with greater ease and clarity, too.

Since that shocking, long-ago coaching session, I've made it my mission to find ways to create a business of ease and flow.

As your coach throughout this book, I'll teach you what I've learned.

The Unexpected Solution

Be warned: what you're going to read in this book is counter-intuitive. In fact, it is downright revolutionary. But, once you learn how to do it, you will never look at overwhelm the same way again.

You've probably tried to handle everything you've got on your plate. If you're like most business owners, you've likely tried some of these things: working even harder so you can finally "get ahead," like blocking out a weekend to catch up on email, or setting up rules about cleaning up your desk or filing your papers; trying different strategies for time management, getting organized, clearing out your clutter, or setting up systems; trying to remember what every magazine on the shelf with the latest hot tip says about how to get organized. For some reason, none of those magazine tips seemed to work as well as promised, or the results didn't last. Pretty soon, you felt just as overwhelmed as when you started.

The truth is, traditional organizing and time management approaches are about encouraging you to fit more in. Do more. Speed up. Squeeze more into your day. Get more efficient so you can cross everything off your to-do list. However, these approaches never stop to consider that maybe you shouldn't do everything on your to-do list. They don't question whether fitting more into your schedule actually makes sense for you. They don't teach you how to make decisions based on what brings you joy and ease *as well as* the results you want. In fact, they don't stop to ask if any of the actions they recommend actually bring better results, period.

When you're overwhelmed, focusing on *getting more done* isn't the answer.

So what *is* the answer?

It's actually very straight-forward: learn how to easily sort what *is* important from what *isn't* – and let the non-important things go – so you can put your energy on what truly matters to you.

The Seven Principles

In this book, I'll teach you seven radical principles designed to help you create a business of ease and clarity:

- **Principle #1: Reconsider being in the know** – Create information breaks in order to recharge your creativity and problem-solving abilities.
- **Principle #2: Get comfortable with time on your hands** – Give yourself plenty of space in your day to connect with your true brilliance.
- **Principle #3: Do less to accomplish more** – Reduce or eliminate up to 80% of what is currently driving you crazy: on your to-do list and your desk, in your email, and on your schedule.
- **Principle #4: Make decisions that are right for you** – Listen to your inner wisdom, which has the answers for you – and ignore the frantic demands of monkey mind.
- **Principle #5: Let go of good to make room for great** – Identify the things that, even though they sound good, aren't working for you the way you'd like, so you can let them go.
- **Principle #6: Blaze your own trail** – Live your life the way you want to – rather than trying to impress the people around you – and instantly remove complication and overwhelm from your life.
- **Principle #7: Lean in to find the buried treasure** – Determine what your busyness has been covering

up, and use what you discover to move into your next breakthrough.

Each principle will teach you a different aspect of creating a business of ease and clarity. You'll stop spending time on emails that don't matter. You'll remove most of the things on your to-do list, or get rid of it altogether. You'll let go of projects and clients and opportunities that aren't a fit for you, leaving plenty of time for those that are. You'll start to listen to your inner wisdom when making business decisions, and cut through the noise to choose what's right for you. You'll be able to hear the inklings and quiet nudges of your soul that have been covered up by a frantic schedule or messy desk. You'll become extremely selective about where you spend your time and energy. You'll be present and powerful with your clients. You'll have time and space in your days for creativity, innovation, and brilliance.

Implement any one of these principles to noticeably improve your business. Practice all of them to transform it.

CHAPTER 1

Principle #1:
Reconsider Being
in the Know

"You already know so much more than you think you know."
—**Elizabeth Gilbert**, *Big Magic*

FoMO: Fear of Missing Out

D r. Dan Herman, a world-renowned authority on consumer behavior, coined the phrase "fear of missing out" in 1996 to define the fear and anxiety of missing out on an exciting opportunity or interesting event that will possibly bring some kind of perceived reward. In other words, FoMO is the sinking feeling that other people must be happier, making more money, and enjoying their lives more than we are.

The FoMO process goes like this:

1. You become aware of the virtually endless possibilities to choose from: events, activities, classes, trainings, opportunities.
2. You believe that you *should* be able to choose as many of those options as you'd like.
3. You see other people doing many different things – things you'd like to be doing, and it looks like they're all highly successful and happy at it.
4. You feel like you're falling behind or failing or missing all the fun, and don't have the time, the money, or the right connections to be part of everything.

When you're caught in the grip of FoMO, all you can see is what you can't do or don't have. Social media, the Internet, and smartphones have given us more access than ever before to information, opportunities, and choices. Plus, we get to watch how other people live – online and in color – all day and all night long.

We text. We tweet. We post on Facebook. We watch news broadcasts. Our email inboxes are flooded with events and activities for us to choose from.

The more options we have, the more FoMO can kick in. We see all the possibilities, and then feel overwhelmed or constrained by the normal limits of life. But we still crave being able to do all the things we want to do, and we want to do them *now*.

In addition, when you're in business for yourself, FoMO can be triggered by your desired success for your business. You may believe it's critical to read the latest industry trends or attend your professional association's events.

You may be driven by a level of anxiety that says you need to keep taking classes and trainings, signing up for webinars and teleclasses, and reading the latest tips and techniques. You're worried that if you don't, you just might miss out on the silver bullet that would skyrocket your success.

More training is always good, right?

But what if it's not?

The High Cost of Staying in the Loop

According to Michael Hogan, PhD, in an October 2015 *Psychology Today* article titled "Facebook and the 'Fear of Missing Out' (FoMO)," FoMO is associated with a variety of negative consequences. In a study using a collective intelligence method to gain further structure regarding the nature of FoMO, Hogan found that participants experienced:

- less overall satisfaction with one's life
- less honesty in what we're sharing online (we often exaggerate how great things are)
- less connection with family and friends
- more jealousy about other peoples' lives
- more personal inadequacy
- more loneliness
- more unfair judgments and criticisms about one's self and others

The flood of information and opportunities will *never* slow down. You will *never* catch up. You will *always* miss out on things. Someone else, somewhere, will always have it better.

In our attempts to exhaust as many options as possible, what we're really exhausting is ourselves.

Just-in-Time Learning

How many newsletters are you subscribed to?

How many blogs do you look at every day?

How many business or self-help books are sitting on your nightstand or in your e-reader, waiting to be read?

How many webinars are on your schedule this month?

How much information is enough?

There's so much content out there; it's ridiculously easy to get information overload. Much of the information we consume is geared toward pointing out problems to be solved or suggesting goals that have yet to be achieved, so if you are spending a lot of your time staying in the loop, you are subtly – or maybe not so subtly – being reminded that you still have plenty of work to do.

When I started my coaching business and signed up for *everything*, I was quickly paralyzed with the onslaught. I had a lot to learn, and it was all great stuff, but I didn't have time to integrate it, so I constantly felt like I was failing. I didn't have any idea how to sort through all of it.

Over the years, I've learned how to leverage the power of *just-in-time* learning instead. The only kind of information I am open to anymore is the information that I will use immediately, that applies to exactly what I'm working on in the moment. In my business, I look at what I want to do next, or what the next challenge is, and if I don't know how to solve it or need more information or support, then and only then do I go out and find help. Just-in-time learning means I let all of the other great information, webinars, teleclasses, articles, and coaching opportunities pass me right by. I don't take a class just because it would be nice to know or because I might need it someday or even because it happens to be interesting. I no longer choose to spend my time that way.

I don't save information for later, either. That would feel like giving myself more and more homework that I would need to do someday.

Instead, I fully trust that when and if I need information, it will come to me in a fresh, new way that is just what I need when I need it. I have found this to be effective 100% of the time.

The 30-Day Information Vacation

How can you tell if you're caught in the grip of FoMO? Or how strong its grip is?

One straightforward, powerful way to learn about your relationship to – and reliance on – information and technology is to unplug for 30 days. Take an information vacation. Turn off the fire hose of input.

Unsubscribe from every newsletter, RSS feed, and online catalog. Delete all the articles with great tips that you've been saving for "someday." Let the free teleclasses and webinars pass you by... even if it's the last time they'll be offered. Toss all the "good idea" folders you've been saving in your filing cabinet, email browser, or computer. Put your business and self-help books on a back shelf. Give social media a pause. Toss your magazines (or donate them to the library), unread.

Want to be even more revolutionary? Turn off the radio when you're in the car. Turn off the TV: the news, the reality shows, the talk shows. Leave your smartphone turned off, or limit your use to necessary phone calls and texts only.

As you start to unplug, you may be surprised to notice how antsy you feel when driving. One way to start calming your inner adrenaline junkie is to drive at the posted speed limits, come to a complete stop at stop signs, and focus on taking full, deep breaths – in and out – as you drive, especially when you're at stop lights and stop signs.

FoMO will likely rear its head, and that's okay. It really is okay to not be in the know.

After the 30 days is up, be intentional and careful about what you choose to bring back in. You may discover that, as wonderful as the idea of ongoing self-improvement is, you actually felt better about yourself when you set aside all the self-help for a month. You might find that you really enjoy driving in the car without the radio, music, or talking.

Taking a vacation from the information flooding in gives you the opportunity to reconnect with your own thoughts, inspiration, and creativity; your connection with nature; friends; and what's really important in your business.

Audio: The 30-Day Information Vacation
I have created a series of audios to support you
on your journey; this audio describes how to tell
if you're caught in the grip of FoMO and what to
do about it. **www.suerasmussen.com/checklist**.

▓ ▓ ▓ ASK YOUR COACH ▓ ▓ ▓

Do you have a question about this chapter? If so, I invite you
to reach out to me at **www.suerasmussen.com/contact**.

CHAPTER 2

Principle #2:
Get Comfortable with
Time on Your Hands

Yes, it's hard to value 'feeling good' when you feel like you're under pressure. But feeling good is part of your work to do. It's a professional responsibility. Otherwise, I ask you, who is doing the work? If you're not nourished and connected to your own flow, what grim pickings are you drawing from?"

—**Tama Kieves**, *Inspired & Unstoppable*

The Seduction of Drama

As much as we may not like to admit it, there is often something slightly thrilling about rushing around doing things, managing the dozens of tasks around us. We jump from one activity to another, then we get interrupted and switch gears all over again.

We feel efficient. We feel important. We feel productive.

We like feeling that way. We like checking things off our lists, and we're proud of being good at handling emergencies as we go from one crisis to another. We get pats on the back for how good we are at it. We get asked for our help, our input, and our advice.

We thrive on the adrenaline high.

Quite frankly, it's often easier to focus on the small emergencies than to work on the important things that might require us to stretch or grow or do things that scare the pants off us.

The drama of a hectic day can be highly seductive. We have plenty to talk about. We can point to this emergency or that issue that we handled, and feel satisfied that we succeeded.

But what is that success, exactly? So we plowed through all of our emails. Gold star? We listened to an interesting podcast. Do we get an A? We spent 45 minutes rearranging our to-do list because it was getting unmanageable, and then 30 minutes on social media. But what about finishing that presentation that's been half-done for six months, or reaching out to call three potential new clients to invite them have coffee?

Reacting to and handling what shows up during the day is one thing; planning and moving ahead on what really matters to you is another thing entirely. If you're not doing the things that are most important to you, it may be because they're getting crowded out by the minutiae of daily life.

Here's the dilemma: as nice as a day of smooth sailing – nothing urgent to handle, the focus on a few important activities, plenty of time – sounds, it can also seem... well... kind of boring.

For many of the women I've worked with, the first thought that comes to mind when taking a 30-day information vacation is suggested is, "But what would I do with all that free time?"

The "Use Time Wisely" Fallacy

What is it about having free time that feels uncomfortable? Why do we think we need to fill up our time?

The concept of using our time wisely has been deeply ingrained in us. We're told that "idle hands are the devil's workshop." Somewhere along the way, we have taken that to mean that we're supposed to use every minute of our time *doing something useful*. Checking something off a list.

Achieving something. If not, we're somehow bad or lazy or not productive enough.

I hear many women saying things like, "I need to be more efficient" and "if I could only get more done."

But what if that's not what "use your time wisely" actually means? What if idleness is not at all the same as breathing room?

Brilliance Needs Breathing Room

The best ideas, the most effective solutions to sticky problems, the most profound inspirations, and the deepest creativity all need plenty of room to breathe. They don't come from hard work; they come from the spaces *in between* the work. The jolt of brilliance in the shower, the perfect phrase that pops into your mind while you're driving, the quiet voice that whispers in your ear while you're taking the dog for a walk, the voice that gives you exactly what you've been looking for while you weren't even thinking about it... all of those gifts show up in the spaciousness, not during the striving.

As a woman in business, you have enormous capacity to impact your slice of the world. But when you are only in *doing* mode, your mind, body, and soul don't have a chance to connect with each other. Your true brilliance shines when you give yourself plenty of room to connect with the deeper parts of yourself that have your best answers.

Instead of working so hard and filling up your time, you'll find many of the answers you're looking for easily... if you have space in the day to be able to hear them. Using your built-in wisdom means making it a priority to *hear* that wisdom.

The more you need to be present in your work – to work with your clients, create or lead presentations, write your book – the more *space* you need in your day. The true value you offer is hardly related to time at all; your real value lies in your ideas, your creativity, and – most importantly – who you are being in your work.

Luckily, you don't need to worry that you don't have enough time. There's plenty to go around.

Audio: Brilliance Needs Breathing Room

On this audio, I show you why your biggest value comes in the spaces in between the work. **www. suerasmussen.com/checklist**.

You've Got Plenty of Time

Right about now you're probably thinking I'm crazy to be telling you that you've got plenty of time. No, I don't know what you've got on your plate right now – how you just brought on a new assistant, or that you're getting your house ready to sell, or that your daughter is getting married next month.

You *do* have a lot on your plate.

But I also do know that you have plenty of time. An overflowing abundance of time. You are rolling in time.

When you say, "I don't have enough time" or "I'm so busy," you're training yourself and your subconscious to never have enough time. When you come from that mindset, no matter which productivity tips or time management software you try, you will never experience lasting change or relief. I know it doesn't sound like a big deal, but how you *think* about time is what runs your entire *experience* of time.

Let's shift your mindset around time. What if you truly believed that you had plenty of time for what most matters to you?

How would you act? What would you choose to do? How would you approach each day?

You can act as if you have all the time in the world to gain the experience of having more of it – because you know your success (and joy) as an entrepreneur depends on it.

Parkinson's Law

Parkinson's Law says that "work expands to fill the time available." When you work for yourself, the "time available" sometimes feels like every hour of every day, seven days a week. When you work all the time, your work expands to fill all of that time.

Leverage Parkinson's Law to give yourself plenty of breathing room. Set working hours and stick to them. See how it feels to leave work at the end of the day. Do this until you feel comfortable *stopping* work at the end of the day.

Then cut your working hours by 30% or 50%. If you started at 40 hours a week, cut your working hours to 20. Look at the most important things to get done during those 20 hours and do them. Ignore the trivial stuff that tends to fill up the workday if you let it.

What would you need to do or set up in order to work half the time you currently do?

▪ ▪ ▪ ASK YOUR COACH ▪ ▪ ▪

Do you have a question about this chapter? If so, I invite you to reach out to me at **www.suerasmussen.com/contact**.

CHAPTER 3

Principle #3:
Do Less to Accomplish More

"Modern life asks us to wear busyness like a badge of honor. Yet the busier we become, the less we're actually creating."

—**Tara Gentile**, *Quiet Power Strategy*

The "Work Harder" Fallacy

How did we get so busy and overwhelmed?

The Protestant work ethic is alive and well. As a society, we seem to believe that we need to sacrifice, work hard, and put in long hours in order to reach the success we want. Maybe that's true for activities in which time equals money, where the time and effort put in typically do equal the results that come out the other end. Or in school, where more effort is typically rewarded with better grades and gold stars for doing extra work.

When you're in business for yourself, however, working harder to get more things done doesn't automatically lead to positive results – even though most of us keep trying for that gold star. Answering hundreds of emails doesn't necessarily lead to a specific, beneficial result. Rearranging your to-do list doesn't automatically mean you achieve a meaningful result. Watching someone else's webinar doesn't necessarily make your business better. Offering more and more products and services doesn't inevitably mean you will be more profitable.

But wait a minute.

Isn't getting more done important? Isn't being more productive a good thing? Isn't "more" better, period?

Well, no. Not exactly.

If the "more" you're getting is more stressed, more overwhelm, more headaches, more issues, and more things that drain your energy, more is not better.

I get it, though. You still want results. Up to now, you thought that if you just worked harder, you'd get better results.

What if "hard work equals success" is a big fat lie?

The Illusion of Being Able to Do It All

As women business owners, we have so many options. So many choices. We have been led to believe that we can do everything and anything we choose. But at what cost to ourselves and to everyone around us?

Do we really *need* to do it all?

What if there were a way to get what we wanted... and do a lot less in the process?

The 80/20 Rule

Over 100 years ago, an Italian economist named Vilfredo Pareto was studying wealth distribution patterns and noticed an interesting imbalance that appeared over and over. In his analysis of data spanning different centuries and across different countries, a small proportion of the total population consistently controlled the majority of the total wealth. His observation about cause and effect, which has become known as the Pareto Principle, or the 80/20 Rule, states that a small number of actions (roughly 20%) almost always leads to the majority of results (roughly 80%). This principle has been shown to apply equally well to many other areas of life. For example, 20% of workers tend to produce 80% of the results, 20% of customers drive 80% of revenue, 20% of computer bugs cause 80% of the crashes, and so on. Closer to home, most of us wear about 20% of the clothes in our closet about 80% of the time.

Just as importantly, the flip side is also true: 80% of actions lead to almost no results at all.

How does this apply to your business?

Knowing the 80/20 Rule can revolutionize your approach to everything: how you handle your email, your time, and your to-do list; the projects you choose and the ones you let go; and the clients you work with and those you don't. The 80/20 Rule is your secret weapon, the principle that can help you instantly cut through overwhelm.

If 20% of your actions lead to 80% of your results, you can apply this principle in all areas of your business and achieve much more by doing much less... simply by noticing whether what you're doing is part of that most valuable 20%. The formula is straightforward: identify the few activities and actions that lead to the best results and do a little bit more of those. You don't even have to increase them very much to have a big impact. For example, if you're currently spending two hours a week on a high-value activity (for our purposes, a "high-value activity" is one that you either highly enjoy or is helping you achieve something you really want), simply increasing that activity by another hour or two per week will likely give you exponentially improved results.

You don't have to work hard or struggle to figure out your top 20%. Just start noticing which activities lift your energy, make you feel happy, or get the best results. Do more of those.

Also notice what drains your energy, makes you feel bad about yourself and your abilities, or makes you feel farther and farther behind. Do less of those things. Cut them out completely, if at all possible.

It's often easier to start by addressing the 80% of things that produce very little value, and begin to remove them immediately, before you focus on your highest 20%.

> Audio: The 80/20 Rule
>
> On this audio, I teach you the powerful principle that can revolutionize how you handle your email, your time, and your to-do list. **www.suerasmussen.com/checklist**.

The Fastest Way to Cut Through Overwhelm

The 80/20 Rule applies to everything in your business:

- your email inbox
- the papers in your filing cabinet
- the stuff on your desk
- the decisions you need to make
- the ideas you come up with
- the time you spend on social media
- the projects you take on

- the newsletters you read
- the trainings and classes you take
- the clients you work with
- the colleagues you associate with

Imagine that 80% of what you do in each of those categories isn't helping your business. Consider that you are getting very little return on that 80%.

What would it be like to let some of that 80% go?

How much time would become available if you got rid of the least valuable 80%? How much energy would that free up?

The solution is not to get better organized, be more efficient, or fit more into your day. The solution is to look at what is most important to you, and get rid of the rest.

The Shortest To-Do List on the Planet

If you're like many entrepreneurs, you've probably tried time management tools, calendar and task software, and tips and strategies to handle your daily schedule. The ideas sound so smart. You write down everything you need to do, want to do, think you should do, and hope to do someday. Your list is long, but at least it's out of your head. You prioritize your tasks into As, Bs, and Cs. You plot them on your calendar.

You spend time every week rearranging and sorting your to-do list. It feels pretty good: you can see everything that you need to do.

But, somehow, you're still frustrated. It's hard to keep up. Many days, your carefully planned schedule goes right out the window.

As wonderful as it sounds, managing time is actually more about speeding up and fitting more into your day than about doing what most matters.

What if the answer were simple instead?

How many items are on your current to-do list? 10? 20? 100?

When you follow the 80/20 Rule, you get a much shorter to-do list. In fact, it's so short you don't even need a to-do list. Instead of focusing on getting more things done, focus on *results*.

When you begin your day, simply ask yourself what is the *one* most important thing you want to get done that day. The *one* thing that will move your business forward. The *one* thing that will make the biggest difference to your results. What's the *one* task that will make your entire week worthwhile?

Then do that one thing before you do anything else. Don't open your email. Don't check social media. Don't attend a meeting. Stop multi-tasking. Just focus on completing that *one* important priority in your day. It might take 20 minutes, or it might take five hours.

Once you've finished that top priority item, before you do anything else, take a moment to consider what else, if anything, you want to do that day. If you have a second major priority, do that next.

Once that's complete, is there a third?

After you've completed your most important activities, you may be done for the day. Remember that the majority of activities fall into the 80% of low-value activities, so there's no need to even do most of them.

So go do something to relax.

You've already done the most important work.

Consider that:

- 20% of actions create 80% of results
- in a 40-hour week, 20% equals one day or eight hours
- the majority of results in the typical work week come from eight hours – or less – of focused effort

A few short hours bring you the most results.

What would your work week look like if you identified the 20% of your time that brings you the most results, and made that time your priority?

You can *accomplish* much, much more by *doing* a lot less than you're currently doing. Your work can become very easy.

How do you decide what's right for you, what your 20% activities are? We'll talk next about using two powerful tools to help you make your best decisions.

▦ ▦ ▦ ASK YOUR COACH ▦ ▦ ▦

Do you have a question about this chapter? If so, I invite you to reach out to me at **www.suerasmussen.com/contact**.

CHAPTER 4

Principle #4: Make Decisions That Are Right for You

"The way you can tell that something lies true north, even though inner-lizard fear says to run from it, is that it feels liberating."
—**Martha Beck**, *Steering by Starlight*

Your One-Two Power Pack

You already have everything you need to make the right decisions for you, every time. I know this because I've seen it while working with thousands of women, and in my own life as well.

You have two powerful tools at your decision-making disposal, and they work beautifully together. First, you have the built-in, carry-it-everywhere tool called your body. Second, you have a quiet inner voice – intuition, gut feeling, God, connection to the Universe – that is available to you anytime you listen.

However, we have been trained since birth to look for information, guidance, and advice outside ourselves. We listen to experts, hire gurus, and ask for other people's opinions. What other people recommend or suggest may be perfect for them, but it might not be right for you at all.

To step into your next level of growth as an entrepreneur, run *everything* through the filter of your own best decision-making tools. Make sure the decisions you make and the actions you take are right for *you*.

How Your Body Talks

The first tool available to you is your own body, which gives you clues all day long. You only need to start paying attention to those clues by noticing the physical sensations you feel in your body.

When you're considering an action or a decision, or simply want to know how your body feels about anything, all you need to do is ask. Then wait for your body to respond. If you pay close attention, your body will typically respond in one of two ways: your body will feel expanded and open, or your body will feel contracted and tight.

If your body expands or opens up in some way, that's your body saying yes. If your body contracts or tightens up, that's your body saying no.

Martha Beck, one of my favorite teachers on the planet, calls these sensations "shackles on, shackles off." When your body is happy, you feel lighter and freer. When your body is not happy, you feel heavy, weighed down, or trapped.

Do you want to experience this effect for yourself?

Think of something in your business that you love: it might be a favorite client, or maybe it's your love of leading groups, or it could be your love of writing. It might be your very favorite pen, the one you love using. Choose something that you already know makes you really happy. Flood yourself with how you feel about this thing you love.

Then check in to see how your body responds.

As you keep breathing, what physical sensations do you notice and where in your body do you notice them?

You might feel this expanded feeling as an opening of your heart or chest, or your shoulders might lift, or you might feel taller. You might feel your cheekbones lift, or you may feel like your head has turned into a balloon filled with air. You might feel the corners of mouth turn upward into a smile.

This is your body giving you a thumbs-up. An open, expanded response is your body is saying yes.

If you don't notice any physical sensations immediately, keep breathing and give your body a chance to respond. Your body might respond very subtly at first, especially if you are new to paying attention to the sensitive feedback you receive.

Now let's see what your body feels like saying no.

Choose something in your business that you just know isn't good for you or that makes you feel bad. It might be someone you never got along with, or a business partnership that isn't working, or something you need to do that fills you with dread or guilt or obligation. Immerse yourself in that thought.

What do you notice? How is your body responding? Where in your body do you feel a response?

Your body has its own unique way of contracting or tightening up.

You might feel this contraction as a knot in the pit of your stomach, or your shoulders may start to feel like they're curling in toward your body, or your throat might start closing, or your neck or shoulders might get tense.

This contracted, heavy feeling is your body's way of giving you a big thumbs-down. That tight, contracted response is the feeling of your body trying to shrink or hide or get away from the thing you imagined.

Your body knows what isn't good for you, and that thing you just imagined is not good for you. Your body is saying no.

You can use your body to give you instant feedback about everything in your business: decisions, activities, projects, clients.

Your body gives you feedback through physical sensations. This works because our bodies are tuned in to our intuition.

Now let's look at the quiet voice whispering in your ear.

Audio: How Your Body Talks

On this audio, I guide you through my very favorite method of accessing your inner wisdom. **www. suerasmussen.com/checklist**.

Your Quiet Inner Voice

In addition to the clues you get from your body, you also have continuous access to a quiet inner voice that knows exactly what is best for you at all times. Even better, your inner voice is always ready to share an authentic, straightforward, easier way to move forward, one that's better than working harder or stressing yourself out.

Your personal, built-in source of information is available to share answers, inklings, ideas, inspiration, and a calming, comforting presence.

This inner voice looks at the bigger picture in your life, seeing farther than you can see. This is the voice that sees beyond how something "looks on paper" and gives you subtle feedback to make decisions on a deeper level. For example, this is the voice that can tell you a business decision you're contemplating is not a good one for you, even though everything seems like it should be a great fit.

All it takes to hear this voice is asking and paying attention.

When you are surrounded by information, it can be hard to hear the quiet whispers of your inner voice. It's easy to miss the messages. Your inner voice doesn't shout, because your inner wisdom knows that all is well, always, and so there is no need to shout.

When you create space in your day, you give yourself the opportunity to hear those quiet messages.

The more you use your built-in wisdom, the more you'll trust yourself and what you're guided to do.

Monkey Mind vs. Your Quiet Inner Voice

How can you tell the difference between your quiet inner voice and the chattering, leaping voice in your head that the Buddhists call "monkey mind"? Monkey mind sounds very different from the voice of your wise self.

Monkey mind is unsettled, indecisive, and loud, urging you to pay attention and fix things *right now*. Monkey mind is flooded with worry and fear, certain that everything is falling apart and that you aren't capable of handling whatever shows up. Monkey mind constantly looks for the worst in every situation.

On the other hand, your quiet inner voice is calm and knows that all is well, always. Your quiet inner voice is reassuring and comforting, supporting you exactly as you are. Your quiet inner voice focuses on simple, authentic answers and guidance, and is always clear on your next step, even if that next step is to take a nap.

Make Only the Decisions Needed Now

Something that has been coming up a lot lately – in my own life, the lives of my friends, and the lives of many of my clients – is the idea that we should be able to untangle all the different possibilities and options of something we're dealing with *up front* and figure everything out well in advance. We try to predict. We want to know what's coming, so we can make the best decisions *now* for something that hasn't shown up yet. We want to know, so we can feel safer, more in control. In other words, we try to make decisions that are way down the road that we don't even need to make yet. We spend a lot of time and energy trying to figure all of this out.

Has that ever actually worked for you? It certainly hasn't worked for me, although that hasn't stopped me from wearing myself out trying at different points in my life.

What if you simply focused on what's right in front of you? What if you only made decisions based on what you know right now?

There is probably an action, or a decision, that you already know to take, one that is right in front of you, something that you can do today.

It's usually something very simple.

It might be to make a phone call that you've been avoiding. You might need to do some research on the place you're considering moving to. Maybe it's time to decide whether to move forward on a project or shelve it for good.

When you give yourself permission to keep your focus on what's happening now, without stressing and worrying and wondering how this moment fits in with the bigger picture, you start connecting with the flow of your own life.

You start listening to your inklings in the moment. You start following your personal energy and rhythms. You receive the guidance you need. You make only those decisions that are right in front of you.

Amazingly enough, time starts becoming your friend. It bends and shapes around what you need. You have plenty of time to do what matters most.

Even better, as you make the decision or take the action that's right in front of you, the next decision, the one you've been struggling with, often becomes clear. I have found that until I do the thing right in front of me, the decision or action after that will not become clear, no matter how much "hard thinking" I put into it.

You can give up the belief that it's your job to *make* it all happen, and surrender to the flow of it unfolding in a way that you couldn't have even imagined. You can let go of needing to know how it's going to turn out, and trust that it will.

Make Courageous Decisions

Be willing to make courageous decisions, especially when you're surrounded by people who are telling you that you're making a huge mistake. If your inner wisdom is telling you to do something, even if you feel fear and the people around you say you're crazy, making that decision is one of the fastest ways to move you and your business forward. On the flip side, *not* making that decision will only serve to keep you stuck, slow down your progress, and keep you feeling overwhelmed and scattered.

Being an entrepreneur who moves through your day with confidence, ease, and clarity often means stepping off the worn path everybody else is walking and blazing your own trail instead.

The more you listen to your inner guidance and trust that you are being led each step of the way, the quieter the external noise becomes. With each courageous decision you make, your decision muscle becomes stronger, and making the next decision gets easier.

▪ ▪ ▪ ASK YOUR COACH ▪ ▪ ▪

Do you have a question about this chapter? If so, I invite you to reach out to me at **www.suerasmussen.com/contact**.

CHAPTER 5

Principle #5: Let Go of Good to Make Room for Great

"By saying no you are able to be available for the right opportunities when they come along."
—**Adelaide Lancaster** and **Amy Abrams**,
The Big Enough Company

Holding on Means Holding Back

We expect children to outgrow their clothes, toys, and books as they move from one phase of life to another. Not only do we expect it, we realize that for children to become healthy adults, they *must* move on from things that served them well as young children but no longer do. Toys that were wonderful for a six-year-old are no longer interesting for a teenager; the teenager has moved past the challenge, interest, and fun of playing with toys designed for younger kids.

You are continually growing, learning, and evolving as well. What worked for you ten years ago – or ten days ago – may no longer work for you today. You may have outgrown it.

It can be really hard to think about letting go of anything – projects you've worked on, ideas you've come up with, programs you created years ago, opportunities that land in your lap – but learning how to let go is a crucial skill for creating a business of ease and clarity.

When we hold on to things that are no longer serving us, those things affect us negatively in a number of ways.

On a practical level, when we keep those things in our life, we need to care for them in some way. We need to spend time on them, make room for them in our space or in our schedule, and invest energy in maintaining them, even at a subconscious level.

On an emotional level, keeping things that no longer serve us can affect our emotions, making us feel everything from overwhelmed to guilty, fearful, or anxious.

On an intellectual level, holding on keeps us focused on thoughts or beliefs that limit us, such as "I couldn't possibly get rid of those notes I wrote 15 years ago. I may need to go back and look at them again someday. I might come up with a bestseller using those notes. All of my good ideas were back in those notes. If I throw them away, I'm throwing away the chance to write a fabulous book." The thoughts we think when we're holding on tightly to something typically focus on the past or the future rather than the present; they tend to be based on fear of some kind. Creativity is thus stifled. Freedom is shackled. We worry that we'll have less or that we'll be giving something up, or that we'll have a big gaping hole where something important once lived.

On a spiritual level, holding on to things that no longer serve us keeps us disconnected from our inner wisdom. Holding on increases confusion and reduces our ability to fully trust ourselves and make decisions that do serve us.

Holding on is about trying to control the flow of life, which includes change, evolution, and the natural fears that come along with change.

Holding on means there is less room for the new to show up.

When you work for yourself, your growth and evolution are critical to your success. It's safe to let go of what no longer serves you.

Letting go is about creating space for what's next, and trusting that the Universe will take care of you.

The Sunk Cost Dilemma

One way we often hold on is based on what we've already invested.

What is it about investing time, money, or effort in something that makes us reluctant to change our minds about it?

I used to coach the clients of a company that specialized in teaching marketing strategies to financial advisors, and one of the comments we heard all the time when clients first started working with us was, "But we don't want to revise our brochures – we just spent thousands of dollars on our new brochures" or "But we just revamped our website." Those materials didn't reflect the brand that we were helping them develop and weren't doing one thing to help grow their business (and in many cases were directly hurting their business), but they still didn't want to change them. Our response was always the same: "No matter how far you've gone down the wrong road, turn around."

That can seem like a tough message to hear.

Continuing down your current path can feel so tempting, simply because it's the path you're already on.

Think of the projects you've continued working on long after they've stopped being enjoyable or profitable, but you had already invested so much into them that you moved forward anyway. Or partnerships with long-time colleagues that just don't seem to fit, but you'd invested years in the relationship.

Moving forward won't recoup what you've already invested. Moving forward isn't likely to improve the situation, either.

When you recognize that you're in the middle of a sunk cost dilemma, stop and breathe. Look at where you've come and where you're going. *It's perfectly okay to change your mind.*

No matter how far you've walked down the wrong road, turn around.

The Butterfly Effect of Letting Go

The butterfly effect is the phenomenon where a small change in one place can have a large effect somewhere else, like a butterfly flapping its wings in Minneapolis might change the weather in Denmark.

As a business owner, you experience the butterfly effect as well. When you are willing to let go of something that isn't serving you, you set in motion changes that start shifting other areas of your business as well.

On a practical level, when you let go, you create an opening for what you do want to come in. You have more room in your space or schedule and you have more energy available to you.

On an emotional level, letting go can feel scary, but also exciting, like looking forward to a much-anticipated trip.

On an intellectual level, letting go is a way of telling ourselves that we are safe, that we can choose to let go, and that something even better is on the way.

On a spiritual level, letting go opens us up to connect with our quiet inner wisdom. We become willing to notice and trust, at a deeper level, in what does bring us joy.

Every time you let go of something that no longer fits who you are now, who you have become, you honor yourself.

Even though the action itself may seem insignificant, in truth, it's *highly* significant. The effect of the action has a ripple effect that goes far beyond the act itself.

I've worked with clients who clean out their filing cabinet, and the next day get an invitation to present in front of a group of people they'd love to work with. They took an action – cleaning out the filing cabinet – that gave themselves permission to move forward in their business. I've also coached clients to delete thousands of old emails and, shortly afterward, cheered them on as they easily raised their rates because they realized how much value they were providing their clients.

I've seen butterfly effects happen enough times that I now fully anticipate them to happen. The specifics of butterfly effects aren't predictable – that's why they are so magical – but they *do* show up every time.

As you make small changes in your space, start to notice what starts shifting in other areas of your life. It helps to keep a notebook or journal – when you track the shifts, you'll start noticing that they are happening everywhere in your life.

When you are willing to let go of things that no longer serve you, you kick off a chain reaction of habits, beliefs, intention, awareness, and focus.

You are making room for great.

How to Tell When It's Time to Let Go

When Michelangelo was asked how he made his statue of David, he is reported to have said, "It is easy. You just chip away the stone that doesn't look like David."

Letting go is about chipping away at what is *not* you to reveal what *is* you: who you are today, not who you were last year.

How do you know what isn't you?

Anything that isn't true to who you are *right now* simply doesn't feel good. This includes projects you've taken on that make you feel exhausted or irritated. It's the folders in your filing cabinet that fill you with anxiety or confusion. It's the things you think you are supposed to be doing, or should be doing, or that you have been told are the "right" way to do things. If they make you feel bad, they aren't you either. Those thoughts in your head – the ones that bring up guilt or pain – those aren't you, either.

The prelude to letting go is often a soft, gentle little voice inside that lets you know something doesn't quite fit anymore. You may start questioning something that used to play an important role in your life. And, once you start questioning, what often comes next is an internal struggle: "Should I keep it?" or "Should I let it go?"

- "Do I stay on the board, or step down as chairperson?"
- "Do I keep offering this program, or do something different?"
- "Do I keep these conference notes?"
- "Do I keep working this way in my business?"
- "Do I love this self-study program I purchased?"
- "Do I enjoy working with this expert?"
- "Do I feel energized and excited when I consider this business model?"

Once you start questioning something, the whispers will continue until you have decided. Often, the answer is to move forward and let go. That's why the voice showed up in the first place. That voice is your first clue that it's time to let go of something so you can make room for what's next.

Once you recognize that something is no longer working for you, it's time to let it go.

Get rid of it. Stop doing it. Bow out.

Not all of the choices to let go will be easy. Sometimes, letting go can feel like the hardest thing in the world to do. Especially when it's something that *seems* good: it looks good on paper, or it used to feel good but no longer does.

It's still safe to let go.

In fact, letting go is the only way to make room for who you are becoming.

Move Some Pebbles to Move a Mountain

Every entrepreneur has an entire mountain resting right behind her, a mountain of challenges, obstacles, concerns, or fears. If she looked right at the mountain, it might seem overwhelming. It could appear too big to handle.

Instead, pick up a few pebbles. Handle the small stuff that's right in front of you.

Clear out the clutter.

Say no to something you don't want, so you can say yes to something you do want.

Have a conversation that you've been avoiding.

Clear off your desk.

Let go of obligations that have been draining your energy.

As you start handling the small stuff – the pebbles – the bigger stuff starts getting handled, too. The mountain starts moving almost on its own, as if by magic.

Picking up a few pebbles starts the ball rolling. The ripple effect begins.

Start easy. Start small.

Trust that you are profoundly influencing what really matters to you.

Make room for great.

▪ ▪ ▪ ASK YOUR COACH ▪ ▪ ▪

Do you have a question about this chapter? If so, I invite you to reach out to me at **www.suerasmussen.com/contact**.

CHAPTER 6

Principle #6:
Blaze Your Own Trail

"You are now free to stop being judged and live the life you've wanted all along."
—**Barbara Sher**, *Refuse to Choose*

Someone Else's Way May Not Be Your Way

Many of my clients are small business owners, entrepreneurs, coaches, or consultants, women who make a living based on their ingenuity, passion, and – just as importantly – on who they are *being* in their business. Here's what they often say:

- "I'm doing everything the experts say, but it doesn't seem to be working very well."
- "I'm not sure exactly why, but I don't like how I'm moving forward with my business."
- "I love what I'm doing, but I just don't know the next step."

There is a lot of information out there about how to build a business, how to get clients, how to improve marketing, how to put together a powerful website, and how to do all the other aspects of being an entrepreneur.

What I've seen is that many small business owners get overwhelmed by all the choices and decisions they need to make every day. In addition, they get used to listening to experts who make their living telling other people how to do things rather than how to listen to their own guidance.

Many times, information, tips, and tools that worked extremely well for that expert may not fit you or your business or your way of doing things at all. You may think that *you* are the problem – if only you could get more motivated, or get organized, or make yourself do what you think you need to do to build your business.

Trying to *make* yourself do something that is not in line with who you really are will never work, at least not for long.

Rather than looking outside of yourself, I invite you to start looking inside yourself.

Get information and advice when you need it, but then run it through your own internal barometer to see if it feels good to you. See if it resonates with you.

Learn how to start recognizing whether something brings you joy or whether it feels "heavy." A great way to tell something feels heavy is that you start avoiding, procrastinating, getting easily distracted, or you get sick.

When you take action in your business in a way that brings you joy, things start to flow, almost as if by magic. The perfect person shows up. An inspired idea comes to you from out of the blue.

On the other hand, when you take action based on what you think you "should" do, things just don't seem to happen the way you'd hoped. It's like the flow is literally being cut off at the source.

Clearing out the things that don't feel like "your way" is one of the best methods I've seen for unsticking things in business and in life in general.

Impress Yourself Instead

In *Simplify Your Life*, Elaine St. James asks, "Have you ever stopped to think about how much energy you spend – and how much you complicate your life – by pretending to be someone other than who you are?"

What if the only person you had to impress was yourself? Would you continue to:

- do the same kind of work
- work with the same kinds of clients
- say yes to things you really wanted to say no to
- drive the same car
- live in the same house
- wear the same clothes
- be married to the same person
- belong to the same clubs or groups
- have the same conversations
- spend time with the same people

When I first started training to be a coach, I took a good look at how I was living my life. Even though, by all outward appearances, I had a great life, I realized that much of what I had, much of what I did, and much of how I acted were based on other peoples' expectations. Actually, it was even worse than that: it was based on what I thought other people *might* be expecting of me.

Step by step, I started creating a life based on how I *truly* wanted to live. Some steps were fairly easy, like letting go of activities that no longer interested me, clearing out lots of stuff that no longer served me, and simplifying my life. Some of the steps were not so easy, like leaving relationships that were not supporting me, moving across the country, completely changing my career, starting a new business, and creating a new community of friends. However, every single step was well worth it.

As you look at your own life and business, you may discover that you have some tweaking to do as well.

Impressing yourself – living your life the way *you* want to, rather than trying to impress the people around you – is one of the most powerful ways to instantly remove complication and overwhelm from your life.

The Unwanted Effects of the Unspoken No

I always find it fascinating that I teach what I most need to learn.

When I was growing up, I worked really hard to be a good girl. I always wanted to make the people around me happy and to not hurt anyone's feelings. One of my mentors used to call me the most polite person she had ever known, and although that might not sound like a negative thing, what it also meant was that I had a hard time saying no and meaning it.

Over the years, I have looked long and hard at the feeling that I'm in charge of everyone else's feelings, and I've seen how it affects every area of my life.

What does this have to do with overwhelm?

I recently noticed my email inbox getting more full and the pile of paper on my desk starting to get bigger.

What? I'm writing a book about clearing out overwhelm, and my own stuff is piling up? Yes, that's exactly what was happening. And, of course, it was the perfect reminder for me.

As I looked at what was really going on with my email and papers, I realized things were piling up because I had half a dozen decisions that were in front of me to act on, but I hadn't made those decisions yet. When I tuned in, I realized that I knew (immediately) what my decision would be on each of them: no.

However, each opportunity, invitation, and request was from someone I admire. Someone I love. Someone I respect.

I didn't want to make anyone feel bad. I didn't want to miss out on a chance to connect with them. Basically, I didn't want to say no, even though saying no was the best way to say yes and be the most supportive *of myself.*

The funny thing was, I *knew* that saying no was the only response I could make, but I put off acting on it. My delay created clutter all over the place. I wasn't sleeping as well as I normally do. When I did sleep, I woke up feeling anxious and stressed. I spent a lot of time and energy avoiding my desk and my computer. I distracted myself with all kinds of activities.

I didn't want to deal with the uncomfortable feelings of saying no. Luckily, I noticed it after a couple of days. Once I had the conversations I had been putting off, I immediately experienced a surge in energy for handling the things that had piled up and quickly handled them.

The funny thing is, saying no can be much easier than we think. You don't need a big explanation when you say no. If you feel uncomfortable saying no, one way to handle it that works beautifully is to create in advance a short list of phrases you can easily use when someone invites you to do something or makes a request of you, so that you can have them on the tip of your tongue when you need to say no. The best responses are short, simple, and elegant:

- "No, thank you."
- "Thank you so much, but I've already got plans." (Even if your plan is to stay at home with a good book.)
- "Thank you for asking, but I'm going to have to say no."
- "Thank you. I appreciate you thinking of me for (volunteering, committee membership, etc.), but my calendar is already full."
- "I appreciate you asking, but I'm creating free time in my schedule right now."

Don't add any loopholes or wiggle room, like "maybe next time" or "unless you can't find anyone else to do it."

True freedom is being able to simply say, "No, thank you," and move on with your life.

Audio: The Unwanted Effects of the Unspoken No

On this audio, I take you through the consequences of saying yes when you'd rather say no, as well as some easy phrases to have on the tip of your tongue when declining an invitation or request. **www.suerasmussen.com/checklist**.

Your Vacation Self, Every Day

One of my clients once told me that she wished she could be her "vacation self" all the time. She's more relaxed on vacation, more able to go with the flow. She is not nearly as concerned about planning *anything* while she's on vacation. She's curious about how the day will unfold, rather than scheduling every minute. She leaves plenty of free time so she can act on what she truly wants to do in the moment.

The day before she leaves to go on vacation, she is excited, full of energy, and focused on getting important things done – without dilly-dallying, indecision, or delay. She wraps up final details on a client project she's been working on, answers important emails (and deletes the rest), and easily follows up on conversations she's been meaning to have. She wants to have a clear head and heart while she's enjoying her vacation, so she handles what's in front of her almost effortlessly.

Her vacation self is *enough*. Her vacation self isn't worried about the next certification she thinks she should get. Her vacation self doesn't wake up in the morning paralyzed by her to-do list.

She really *likes* her vacation self. She's fun to hang out with. When she's on vacation, she lives moment by moment, enjoying new sights and food and things that are different from home, rather than rehashing something that happened in the past or worrying about the future. She's *present*.

What if your vacation self is the right person to run your business?

What would that look like? More importantly, what would that *feel* like?

■ ■ ■ ASK YOUR COACH ■ ■ ■

Do you have a question about this chapter? If so, I invite you to reach out to me at **www.suerasmussen.com/contact**.

CHAPTER 7

Principle #7: Lean in to Find the Buried Treasure

"This is where the real gold lies, if you're brave enough to mine it. The path is a courageous one. Only real heroes survive."

—**Lissa Rankin**, *The Anatomy of a Calling*

Your Next Breakthrough

Overwhelm is a combination of what comes at you from the outside and what's happening on the inside. Often, distractions are there to keep you from *noticing* what's happening on the inside.

I invite you to start noticing.

Your next breakthrough lies within those feelings and thoughts; they currently drive your life, often without you being fully aware of it. When you are willing to start noticing, then you can make different choices.

I'm always excited when a client tells me she's stuck or overwhelmed or freaked out. She may not like how it feels, but I know that she's ready for a major breakthrough if she's willing to explore what's there.

You are being called to step deeper into your authentic self. It's safe to go there.

When You Feel Confused, Go Within

When I'm feeling confused or stuck about something in my life, I am very tempted to go into my intellectual "figure it out" mode.

I have that mode down to a science. I get out my clipboard with lots of paper. I take out my favorite pens. I write long lists, with pros and cons. I create plans. I try to force the answer to come. I also go searching outside myself for the answer; it's really tempting to believe that some other expert will have my answer. It feels very productive to be *doing* something. Anything.

Then, in the process of trying hard to figure it out, I start to notice how overwhelmed I feel. I get even more confused. Things pile up while I'm trying to figure it out.

Here is what I have discovered: when I'm feeling stuck about something, that is *not* the time to try to figure it out. If the answer is supposed to be found, it's actually pretty easy to find.

Any time I catch myself *trying* to figure something out, that's my big red flag that it's time for me to stop and go within.

By "go within," I mean reconnect with my inner wisdom. Get still. Be quiet. Do nothing. Play. Go to the movies. Do something wonderful to take good care of myself. It also means letting go of trying to find the answer (that's the hardest part for me).

When I do that, though, the answer I most need shows up on its own. I'll either have an inspiration at a completely unexpected moment, or someone will call with exactly what I need, or something will fall into my lap at the perfect time.

Working hard to try to figure something out always creates overwhelm for me. And all that hard work never goes anywhere – it never creates the answer I was looking for anyway.

So, the next time you feel confused or stuck, rather than trying to force an answer, consider reconnecting with yourself. Find your own peace. Connect with your inner wisdom.

Spend some quiet time in nature. Take a long walk, or sit at a picnic bench under a lovely shaded tree. Move on with your life.

Allow the answer to come to you on its own, in its own time.

Because it will.

Follow the Inklings, Even When They're Scary

You receive whispers and inklings and sparks of inspiration all day long, each and every day. Some are simple, like "Take a right turn now and try that new coffee shop" (when, truth be told, you're already late and the last thing on your mind is stopping for coffee).

Some inklings seem bigger, like "Move across the country" (when you just painted your living room) or "Go work with dolphins" (when the closest dolphins are 1,000 miles away) or "Take a month off" (when you're overwhelmed and don't think you could possibly slow down for even an hour).

The actions your inner wisdom suggests will often seem inconvenient. Irresponsible. Terrifying.

But those inklings are vitally important. You receive them for a very good reason. You likely will not know what that reason is, especially in the moment. The truth is, you don't need to know the reason. You don't need to be able to see the five-year outcome (yes, I know you'd really *like* to see the entire picture before you decide to take that leap of faith).

Leaps of faith don't work that way. You fling yourself off an imaginary cliff every time you act in faith, trusting that a net will appear, or that you will sprout wings, or that the ground will only be six inches below you.

Taking a leap of faith means that you trust yourself – and the Universe – enough to be able to handle whatever that path might bring. Leaps of faith are always about stretching you and growing you and supporting you along your journey.

In my experience, there are two powerful ways to notice and follow inklings:

- Follow anything that brings you authentic joy. Note that real joy is different from a hyped-up, overly high feeling of excitement. Authentic joy is quiet; it feels like all is well with you and the world.

- Follow anything that makes your body relax, even when your head is filled with fear. When I'm working with clients, we look for that expansive, open sensation in the body. When you have that open feeling in your body, it's safe to follow it, even if you're scared.

Your inkling might not make any sense at all to your rational mind. It might seem crazy. You might have the feeling that something big is coming, but you're not sure you want to take the action you feel guided to take.

When you try to ignore your inner inklings, life can get overwhelming. When you turn away from your own guidance, you often complicate your life without meaning to.

On the other hand, when you follow inklings, you will often immediately feel a sense of peace or "right-ness," even in the midst of fearing the unknown.

Every time you take one step forward to follow where you're guided to go, the next step will naturally show up.

Your Very Own Archeological Dig

I tell my clients that clearing out their overwhelm or clutter is like going on an archeological dig into their life. An archeological dig is simply about exploring what's there, without judgment. You can never be quite sure what you'll find, and you'll always learn something interesting.

I was working with someone who felt motivated to go through her filing cabinets, email, and computer documents... and she was completely surprised at what she uncovered. She found 20 half-completed versions of a book she had been working on for the past year – versions she'd begun and then stopped working on without finishing.

Until she started going through her files, she hadn't realized that she had not finished any of the versions. They had been filed under different headings, under completely unrelated subjects, and she hadn't even noticed that she'd been repeating the same writing over and over and over again.

She kept telling herself that she needed more information, or that she needed to take a break from that particular writing because it simply wasn't flowing, or any number of other reasons in the moment.

When she took a good look at why she was getting bogged down, she could see that 20 partially-finished versions meant that her mind was split in twenty different directions. Plus, every time she left another version incomplete, she gave herself the unintended internal message of "I can't complete it."

After she saw all of those partial versions and realized what was going on, she felt energy drain out of her like water flowing out of a sieve and she started clearing out those old versions. Delete, delete, delete. Shred, shred, shred.

What had felt stuck and overwhelming now felt like freedom. Ease. Flow. The very next day, she had the clarity and insight to move forward – and she soon finished writing her book.

As you go on your personal archeological dig through your stuff, pay attention to what you find.

Notice the patterns.

Watch what happens to your energy.

See where your emotions flare.

Pay attention to what makes you feel like you're in the flow, and what makes you feel stuck and blocked and overwhelmed.

You have the opportunity to learn everything about your beliefs, where you get stuck, and where you experience pure ease and flow, simply by going on your own personal archeological dig into your stuff.

Dare to Be Average

We often hesitate to try something new for fear of failing. We forget that failure is a completely natural part of our growing process. If all babies learning to walk quit after the first tumble, we'd all be leading pretty sedentary lives. But we were born willing to try, to stretch, to grow… and to stumble along the way. It's all part of the journey.

Somehow, we became conditioned to play small and safe. We learned to be careful, to look good, to worry about making mistakes. How much simpler life would be if our mistakes and growing pains were celebrated along with our successes.

I sometimes catch myself thinking that I "should" know how to do something I've never done before. I've learned to step back then, to put things in perspective, and to give myself a huge break. When I do, I am much more excited and willing to step right in.

I bet you could easily think of memorable times in your life when you did something new, difficult, challenging, or scary. Maybe nothing about the experience went perfectly, yet you became a different person because of it. Think of learning to write the alphabet, experiencing your first kiss, or giving birth to your first child.

One summer, during my college years, I was an exchange student and lived with a host family in the tiny town of Sillé-le-Guillaume, in France. One day, some friends invited me to participate in a four-person team rowboat race that would take place the following week.

I was by no means an expert rower, and I had no team and no time to do anything resembling training. And we would compete against teams of men.

I could hear all the reasons to politely decline yelling in my head. Yet it sounded like a lot of fun, so I heard myself say yes to the invitation.

Of course, right away, fear set in. Would I make a complete fool of myself? Luckily, I chose to move forward anyway.

I immediately contacted several other American friends who were staying with host families in nearby towns and asked them to be my teammates. My host mother named us *The American Express*. My teammates traveled to town the day of the race. They were apprehensive, yet enthusiastic.

The race was complete chaos. A couple of the women on my team had never rowed. It was windy and rainy and cold, and the lake was choppy. We decided to simply give it our all and have a good time. We didn't worry about being any good. We didn't worry about failing. I mean, we were in France, in a boat race, in the rain, hanging out with a bunch of friends. We were cheered and supported and teased and encouraged all along the way by the fans who came out to watch the race. We laughed and pulled on the oars and told stories and had a great time.

What felt like a hundred laps later, we arrived at the finish line, soaking wet, exhausted, and blistered... in second to last place.

We were totally average when it came to winning the race. In every other sense that mattered, we succeeded beyond our wildest dreams. We were ecstatic. We'd done it. We'd finished the race. We were four completely happy, exhausted women. To this day, it's one of my very favorite memories of my time in France.

Dare to be average. Be willing to try something new, maybe something you've always wanted to do, and give yourself permission to do it "not perfectly." When you've done it, ask yourself if you enjoyed what you were doing, even if it was nowhere near perfect. If so, go ahead and do it again. Or do something else new.

You'll either improve, or you'll enjoy yourself so much it won't matter.

■ ■ ■ ASK YOUR COACH ■ ■ ■

Do you have a question about this chapter? If so, I invite you to reach out to me at **www.suerasmussen.com/contact**.

CHAPTER 8

What Could Go Wrong?

"Success is not a solitary journey. Ask any six-figure woman."
—**Barbara Stanny**, *Secrets of Six-Figure Women*

The Rider, the Elephant, and the Path Run the Show

In their book *Switch: How to Change Things When Change Is Hard*, Chip and Dan Heath look at the reasons it often feels so hard to making lasting changes in our lives.

The reasons can be surprising.

Psychologists have discovered that we have two different minds that compete for control all day long: our rational mind and our emotional mind.

This competition for control of our actions is described beautifully by Jonanthan Haidt in *The Happiness Hypothesis*, as our rational mind (the Rider) sitting on top of our emotional mind (the Elephant).

The Rider is constantly on the lookout for clear directions and a clear destination. In other words, the Rider wants a plan. And if there is no specific plan of action, the Rider will analyze and think and over-think and then agonize and back around again.

The Elephant is all about motivation and action. If the Elephant doesn't want to do something, it won't take action – no matter how much the Rider insists. If you have ever slept in when you told yourself you'd get up early, or piled up more papers on the desk right after you vowed to get organized for good this time, you've experienced the Elephant running the show.

The Path that the Elephant and Rider travel is equivalent to the environment and how well it is set up to support the desired action. If there seem to be insurmountable obstacles on the Path, if there is not enough support, or if the environment keeps the undesired behavior firmly in place, it's going to be really hard for the Rider and Elephant to stay on that Path.

But the opposite is also true.

When you get the Rider, the Elephant, and the Path all on board and supporting the same desired action, change can be surprisingly fast.

Here's how to do that:

1. Make sure the Rider is clear about what needs to be done, and be very specific. Choose a small number of actions that are critical to success, and ignore all the rest.

2. Get the Elephant on board by connecting with the *feeling* of what the Elephant wants, and by taking small, bite-sized action steps that don't trigger resistance or fear.

3. Set up the Path to make the change easy. Make the environment supportive and instill simple habits that become routines.

You'll stir up the Rider, the Elephant, and the Path when you work with the principles in this book. Make no mistake: the principles in this book are radical. They're not for the faint of heart. But you were led to this book for a reason. You're ready for radical. You're ready to make the shift from overwhelmed to calm, confident, and successful. If you implement what you've learned in this book, you'll make that shift. As you shift, the

Rider, the Elephant, and the Path will synchronize more and more.

Let's face it, lots of people who read books don't follow all the recommendations. They pick and choose, they combine things, they stop and start, they don't see results right away, they give up... and everything goes back to how it was. I don't want that to happen to you, so I'm going to share with you what's likely to happen and the problems and pitfalls people run into when they try to implement the ideas in this book.

Let's look at some of the obstacles that are likely to show up on your path.

Things Feel Worse Before They Get Better

One thing I've noticed in the years I've been coaching is that whenever a client makes a decision and a commitment to make significant changes in her life, initially things can seem to get worse before they get better.

I call this the "muddy waters" phase.

It's just like what happens at the end of your driveway after there's a long rain. The runoff of water and dirt collects in a puddle at the base of the driveway. The water in the still puddle looks fairly clear and calm. However, if you take a garden hose and spray away the puddle, all the mud and soil that collected at the bottom gets stirred up and things start looking pretty messy – until the water from the hose has had a chance to wash all the muck away.

Big change can be like this.

When you get started on tackling something you want to change, the mud and dirt start to show. Things feel messy for a while.

As unpleasant as this may sound, going through the "muddy waters" phase is actually a very good thing. It means you're starting to get to the heart of the matter. You're on the right track. You're getting your hands dirty. You're doing the work. In fact, this is the *only* way to do the work.

Eventually, the water will wash clean again.

The Flood Keeps Coming

When my clients implement Principle #1: Reconsider Being in the Know, it typically feels like a shock to their system. They often had no idea how much information was inundating them: newsletters, free teleseminars, news broadcasts, podcasts, programs they're taking, or blogs they're reading. One cornerstone of the program I do with clients is a 30-day information vacation, and one of the first things program members do is unsubscribe from everything they're currently subscribed to.

When they do that, they notice how *natural* it had become to jump online and search for things on the

Internet all day long, especially because technology allows us to be connected at any time we choose.

The amount of information available is not going to slow down. Information is wonderful. It's fun, it's helpful, it's entertaining. Colleagues will tell you about articles you need to read. Friends will forward things you "need to know." The level of information you currently access can feel so normal.

You can create a new normal. You can experience freedom around information: enjoy it while you want or need it, and create plenty of boundaries around it so it doesn't overtake your life.

Being very deliberate about what kind of information – and how much of it – you access takes ongoing care and intention. Otherwise, you can easily find yourself inundated again.

You Feel Guilty, Anxious, and Bored

When my clients start practicing Principle #2: Get Comfortable With Time on Your Hands, one of the most common challenges that comes up right away is how *uncomfortable* having "free" time feels. They are surprised to notice that although they like having the free time, they also miss the distractions. They constantly feel the urge to fill their time, to get online, to reach for their smartphone. They don't quite know what to do with themselves without instant access to technology or information. They feel *bored*.

I remind them that overwhelm is a combination of external inputs – like the email inbox that keeps filling up day after day, and internal drives – like boredom, guilt, anxiety, or stress. When you start to peel back the layers of the external inputs, the internal drives become a lot more noticeable.

Without a way to address the internal feelings and experiences, you'll fill that time right back up, whether you're conscious of doing so or not.

You'll need to be committed to handling the overwhelm at a deep level, rather than simply trying to address the symptoms. Otherwise, that overwhelm is going to recur. Your to-do list will get long again. You'll bring back the distractions.

Our Culture Worships Busy

When one of my clients recently started to integrate Principle #3: Do Less to Accomplish More, she commented that "The idea of using the 80/20 Rule for my business is blowing my mind. I love it, and at the same time I'm holding on tightly to everything on my to-do list." Working together, we took a good look at which actions were important for accomplishing what she wanted to achieve, and which actions were inadvertently side-tracking her.

Your strongly ingrained work ethic will likely rear its head. As a culture, we highly encourage being busy, working through long checklists, and being more and more productive.

You'll probably feel guilty that you're not busy enough. You might worry that you won't accomplish anything. You may watch other people scurry around, fitting more and more into their days. You'll no longer be part of the "busy" culture, so you'll have less to commiserate with when everyone else complains about how crammed their schedules are.

You'll wonder if you're crazy.

At those moments, it will be crucial to have the support of other people in your life who know that doing less in order to accomplish more is not only possible, but is an easier, more powerful way to operate.

Otherwise, it's really easy to get sucked back in to trying to fit more and more into your day.

You Are Surrounded by People With Opinions

As you begin implementing Principle #4: Make Decisions That Are Right for You, you might notice how often other people tell you what to do. Some are people you've hired to tell you what to do. Some might be friends or family. Others might be colleagues who want to share something that has worked for them, or things they think that you should try.

There is no shortage of people who have opinions about how you should run your business and your life.

But nobody knows you the way you know you. Nobody else knows what really makes you tick – not even your nearest and dearest.

To make the decisions that are right for you, it's crucial to run all of those opinions and suggestions and great ideas from other people through your inner barometer. You may need to be reminded – and often – to check in with yourself. The more surrounded you are by people who encourage you to follow your own guidance, the better.

Otherwise, you'll likely slip back into looking outside yourself for your answers... and what you'll get are answers that are best for the person giving them.

Clutter Tries to Trick You

Oh, the angst that Principle #5, Let Go of Good to Make Room for Great, brings up.

It sounds like such a good idea. Easy, even. Make room for great. Let go.

In practice, it's one of the most challenging principles.

We tell ourselves all kinds of stories about why we hold on to things, whether it's a pile of stress-ridden paper on our desk, activities that fill us with dread, or clients who drain our energy.

Clutter will try everything possible to trick you into believing it's *not* clutter.

I bet you've experienced this yourself. When you catch yourself telling very creative and inventive stories about why you need to keep something, you can be certain you're dealing with some form of clutter.

Things that bring you joy and raise your energy don't need sophisticated explanations or convincing stories. But clutter does.

When I'm working with a client and she's giving me a creative reason about why she needs to keep something, I suspect we're dealing with one of her personal blind spots. She can't see it until I point it out. Then it's as if a curtain is drawn back, the hypnotic pull is interrupted, and she can make a choice based on what *will* serve her.

As you bump into your own blind spots, it's important to have support from someone who isn't buying into the stories you're telling yourself about why you need to hold on.

You Experience Pressure to Fit In

When my clients live Principle #6: Blaze Your Own Trail, they start to recognize areas in their lives where they have been feeling the pressure to fit in, to be liked, or to compromise themselves. They worry about keeping up with other entrepreneurs. They worry that other people won't like them if they do what they *really* want to do. They don't want to make other people mad. Instead of saying no they say... maybe.

Stepping back from the noise to reconnect with what *you* want is necessary for creating a business that works for you.

Endless Distractions Tempt You

When you're trying to reach your next breakthrough, you are absolutely, positively going to run into fears, obstacles, and doubts. Principle #7, Lean in to Find the Buried Treasure, is about discovering how to move forward anyway – because the gold lies right on the other side of those fears, obstacles, and doubts. They can be your biggest teachers, if you're willing to let them.

In the midst of fear and doubt, it's so tempting to fall back into the *relief* of distractions. It's so easy to focus on busy work. The information superhighway – and getting overwhelmed again – has been a habit.

It can *seem* to feel better to distract yourself than it does to do something that scares you. As a result of our work together, one of my clients recently told me she was able to see – for the first time – how she had been using what was going on in her life as an excuse to avoid her business. Now she deeply trusts herself and her decisions as she moves forward.

You will need regular reminders that you can do what you're scared to do. You can trust your inner guidance. You can follow your inklings. You can try things you've never done before. In fact, each of those is a requirement for stepping into the role you're being invited to live.

▪ ▪ ▪ ASK YOUR COACH ▪ ▪ ▪

Do you have a question about this chapter? If so, I invite you to reach out to me at **www.suerasmussen.com/contact**.

CHAPTER 9

Everyday Ease, Confidence, and Clarity

"The experiences that reflect luminosity are those based on actions taken with clarity, focus, ease, and grace."
—**Maria Nemeth**, *Mastering Life's Energies*

R ight now, you might not be able to clearly see what your life will be like when you've cleared out the overwhelm and distractions.

I can see it, though.

I've helped thousands of women who are like you – overwhelmed, wanting to focus less on their desks and more on making room for what really matters.

I *know* you can do it.

You can create a life where you wake up with plenty of time to do what you want, where you aren't working nearly as hard, and yet you accomplish a lot more, with ease.

The fog is gone. The adrenaline has quieted.

You feel calm and confident.

Getting Started

To start creating your life of ease and flow, look at where you're getting your best results and your most enjoyment and put your energy there first. Then eliminate everything else as much as you can – that will likely be 30 to 80% of what you're currently doing, so you'll immediately free up a bunch of time.

Get comfortable with all of that free time. You'll be inclined to fill it, so be aware of that temptation. Enjoy it. Revel in it. *Use it to enjoy yourself.* Take an information vacation. Unsubscribe. Unplug. Notice your inner drive to re-engage.

Practice using your built-in decision-making tools to support yourself as you decide what's important and what's not. Keep letting go of what's not important. Make room for great.

Do things your way. Say no and say it often. Be willing to be revolutionary.

Lean in to doubts, fears, or obstacles. You're on the brink of breakthrough.

When you integrate any of these principles, you remove a layer of overwhelm, you build a new muscle – and you continue to get stronger every day.

How Do *You* Approach Change?

Some people love the do-it-yourself approach to making major changes, experimenting and trying different things, even if it takes longer that way. If that's you, I hope you use this book as your workbook, guide, and map and put each principle into practice in a way that really works for you and gets great results.

Or you may find it easier – and faster – to implement lasting change with some support, guidance, and encouragement. If quick and easy is what you want, I'm here to help.

If you're ready to clear out the overwhelm and start living each day with ease, confidence, and clarity, you can schedule a strategy session at **www.suerasmussen.com/strategy-session**.

During our session we'll talk about what you *really* want, what kind of overwhelm you're dealing with, and how your overwhelm affects you and your business. We'll uncover hidden challenges and blind spots that may be sabotaging you, and we'll identify at least one next step for you to take.

Acknowledgments

It takes a village to write a book. I feel deep appreciation and gratitude for all of you in my village.

Thanks to Susan Klein, my very first coach, who shocked – and delighted – me to the core by coaching me to stop taking the hard road. You kicked off the seismic shift in my brain that continues to this day.

Thanks to Stephanie Miller, extraordinarily gifted intuitive, for rocking my world by telling me I'd be just fine without a to-do list.

Thanks to Mom and Dad, for always encouraging my love of reading and learning. You're the best.

Thanks to every coach, mentor, guide, and author I've known throughout my journey. This book would double in length if I listed you all. You have my endless love and gratitude.

Thanks to my amazing group of friends. You lift me up, hold me, challenge me, and inspire me.

Thanks to Grace Kerina and the Difference Press team, for making the process of writing and publishing a book so much fun.

Thanks to Angela Lauria, publisher extraordinaire, whose straightforward manner and spot-on coaching are forces to be reckoned with. I knew the moment I read your book that I wanted to work with you, and the experience has been better than my wildest dreams.

Thanks also to every client and student who has gifted me by showing up, playing full out, and teaching me every step along the way.

About the Author

 Sue Rasmussen helps business owners let go of what holds them back in their businesses and lives – overwhelm, procrastination, stress, or clutter – so they can achieve the success and make the difference they really want. She's a professional coach and author who has worked with over 6,000 small business owners, entrepreneurs, coaches, and consultants in 29 countries since 1998. Sue uses a combination of practical action, spiritual wisdom, and guided self-discovery to help her clients achieve deep, lasting transformation.

Sue's work has been featured in *Success* magazine, *Women Entrepreneurs* magazine, and on NBC's *Today* show.

Website: www.suerasmussen.com
Email: sue@suerasmussen.com

Thank You

Thanks so much for reading. The fact that you've gotten to this point in the book tells me something important about you: you're ready. You're ready to shift out of overwhelm. You're ready to experience clarity and sanity in your day.

To support you in clearing out the overwhelm, I created some special bonuses just for you, starting with a series of audios that you can use in the heat of the moment when it feels like you've got more on your plate than you can possibly handle. You will also receive the **Business Sanity Checklist**, a simple self-assessment to help you get crystal-clear about which red flags you need to watch for when your desk – and your business – is driving you crazy.

You can get your copy of the audios and the **Business Sanity Checklist** at **www.suerasmussen.com/checklist**.

Morgan James
Speakers Group

We connect Morgan James published
authors with live and online events
and audiences whom will benefit
from their expertise.

Morgan James makes all of our titles available
through the Library for All Charity Organizations.

www.LibraryForAll.org